WALLS

WALLS
Deidi von Schaewen

PANTHEON BOOKS, NEW YORK

To Else Strobelt, Peter Harnden, Michael Warren

All rights reserved under International and Pan-American Copy-right Conventions. Published in the United States by Pantheon Books, a division of Random House, Inc., New York, and simulta-neously in Canada by Random House of Canada Limited, Toronto. Originally published in Holland as **Muren** by Andreas Landshoff Productions B.V., Amsterdam; in England by Thames and Hudson, Ltd., London; in France as **Murs** by Les Presses de la Connaissance, Paris; in Germany as **Mauern** by DuMont Buch-verlag, Cologne; and in Japan as **Kabe** by Bijutsu Shuppan-Sha, Tokyo. All rights in all countries: Andreas Landshoff Productions B.V., Amsterdam.

Library of Congress Cataloging in Publication Data
Schaewen, Deidi von, 1941–
Walls.
  1. Photography, Artistic. 2. Walls—
Pictorial works. I. Title.
TR654.S33 1977   779'.4'0924   77-1982
ISBN 0-394-41039-4
ISBN 0-394-73390-8 pbk.

Grateful acknowledgment is made to W. W. Norton & Company, Inc., and The Hogarth Press, London, for permission to reprint the specified excerpt on pages xi-xii from pages 46-48 of **The Note-books of Malte Laurids Brigge,** by Rainer Maria Rilke, translated by M. D. Herter Norton. Copyright 1946 by W. W. Norton & Company, Inc. Copyright renewed 1977 by M. D. Herter Norton. Grateful acknowledgment is also made to Herb Lubalin for permission to reprint the selection which appears on pages v-vi.

Manufactured in Japan by Dai Nippon, Ltd., Tokyo
First American Edition

Foreword

Walls were created to house people, shelter them against the elements, and protect them from oppressors. Over the ages their original purpose has become subverted. In recent years walls have become a means to shut in or shut out people and ideas. These walls, by Deidi von Schaewen, are different. They represent a fascinating means for dispensing information. They have, magically, opened up an entire avenue of aesthetics that stimulates discerning people, creates ideas and insights that reflect cultures and conditions that are, unfortunately, slowly disappearing from the face of the earth. As a graphic designer, with a particular interest in letterforms and their application to surfaces, I am particularly enthralled with the graphic images so aptly captured by Deidi von Schaewen. Our highly sophisticated printing techniques have robbed contemporary posters and billboards of a textural quality that can be achieved only by the reaction of time and the elements (rain, snow, sunshine) on a painted surface. The marvelous della Francesca, weathered, fresco-like appearance of faded paint, cracked plaster, crumbled brick and cement, plus the three-dimensionality of old windows and doors appearing, mysteriously, through images of faces, bodies, and letterforms, provides an extra dimension that boggles the mind of the aesthete, a phenomenon that cannot be reproduced by contemporary printing methods on the uninspiring surface of a piece of coated paper. What strikes me as significant in these photographs is, firstly, Deidi's ability to discern and select, out of the thousands that are available for the eye to see, only those walls that have become artistically credible. And secondly, the volume of work she has created in this area surpasses anything I have seen in the past, not only for its proliferation but for the consistent photographic and design quality, all of which attests to her ability as a graphic designer as well as a talented photographer. This new book of walls is, probably, the most important document on a subject that surrounds people, a subject that they look at every day, but never see. This book will open many eyes to what has happened in the past, and how it reflects upon the future. I remember, a

few years back, seeing the words, "Kilroy was here" embla-
zoned on walls in a myriad of graphic styles. It should have
read "Deidi was here … there … and everywhere."

Herb Lubalin

Author's Notes

Walls: Famous buildings are most people's landmarks. Mine are walls: they are my inner map. Any wall interests me for its intrinsic quality: be it traces, different materials, lettering, advertising, people's idiosyncrasies, decoration, destruction. I always know where the walls are, or where they stood whenever they have been destroyed or painted over. The early publicity was gigantic in scale and gave color to the streets; the inscriptions made dull façades come alive.

The walls in the book are all houses' walls—not enclosing walls, not separating walls, like those of prisons or the Berlin Wall. My interest lies in architecture, environment, painting, graphic design, as well as photography.

Memory: I don't remember Berlin from my childhood. I left it at the age of two, during the war, and grew up in the country. But my favorite pastime was drawing "cuts" of houses with the life going on inside exposed. Maybe I did remember.

First picture of a wall: 1962. While a student at the Hochschule für Bildende Künste and painting in Berlin, I was watching a friend in the darkroom, and the growth of a photographic print out of nothing fascinated me so much that I decided then and there to start photography. I bought a 6x6 Ikaflex for 80 DM and within the first few days I photographed a wall (page 55). I went back two months later to shoot some details—the men running out of the wall, the priest on a bicycle—but a new house had covered the wall. I then knew that I would be photographing walls for a long time. I then discovered them all around me.

How and where: My researches are usually systematic, with a map, street by street, and other times haphazard: on foot, by bicycle, by bus, by car, by moped. Sometimes friends tell me about a wall they have seen. I just found my first Bébé Cadum wall, in Paris, after three years' looking (page 91); I spent days in an area where a friend told me he had seen one, only to find it by accident in a completely different spot.

I photographed walls wherever I lived—Berlin, Barcelona, New York, Paris—and on trips through France, Spain, Italy,

Belgium, England, and Jamaica. Trips usually took me quite long because I stopped whenever I saw an interesting wall. My trips have become faster now because most walls are gone: painted over in grey, yellow, and olive green and carrying posters. The same stuff for hundreds of kilometers.

Destruction walls: They are likely to be the shortest-lived walls. That might be why they are often so intense. They are the <u>objets trouvés</u> of the cities, the unintended artwork, the short-lived monuments, accidental and popular statues, memories. I wish that some could be kept as they are…or that such walls could be re-created.

Time element: It is in all the photographs, but sometimes it becomes more important, as in the case of the Blendol Lady in Berlin (pages 49–51). When I saw her again ten years later, I discovered a window cut out through her chin. Or the case of the Barcelona destruction wall (pages 130–135), which I found still standing seven years later. Some remnants of the posters, cabaret playbills, and newspaper clippings with which someone had decorated his room were still there. Seven years before, I had thought of ripping the collage off for safe keeping; now I was happy I had not done so. Or the more recent case of the hole cut by Gordon Matta-Clark through a house in Les Halles of Paris, which became a wall in a matter of days: the time of the destruction of a house (pages 122–123). Or the brick wall of an old three-story tenement in the Chelsea section of New York (page 121), which collapsed one night, leaving all the rooms with their tenants still inside suddenly exposed. A short time later, the wall was rebuilt and the people moved back in again.

Yesterday and today: I once approached the men in charge of advertising at Saint-Raphaël, Dubonnet, and Byrrh and suggested that something be done about their old advertising walls. A national contest, maybe, around photographing those walls. The answer was: "We are in 1973. We want to be modern. We would prefer that those dirty old walls did not exist any longer."

Docteur Pierre: I was still able to find twelve existing walls of Docteur Pierre in and around Paris (pages 82–87). I put them together in a portfolio of photographs, and wanting to include some data in it, I did research in <u>mairies</u>, prefectures, libraries, and universities. After three months I came up with the birth certificate of Dr. Pierre-Alphonse Mussot, born in Paris, 1801; his student papers and his doctoral thesis, 1833; the history of the factory which he founded in 1837; a booklet for the use of his salesmen—this booklet is a real "pop art" object with photographs of his second factory (the building still stands in Nanterre); multi-scale color ads of his products; and an engraving of Docteur Pierre himself as it is on the walls! I also found the last empty tubes of his carmine toothpaste as well as the final stock of plastic carryout bags.

Bristol-Myers bought the factory in 1967. They discontinued manufacture of Docteur Pierre's toothpaste in 1969, at which time the business's archives were thrown away. The date of the painting of Docteur Pierre, which was the original goal of my search, remains, so far, unknown to me.

Docteur Pierre began making tooth powder because he often noticed, when he went to the Paris Opéra, that the women singers' teeth were lousy.

I photographed one Docteur Pierre in summer, fall, and winter (page 83). I was waiting for spring and for the ivy to start growing again over his face on the wall, but when I got there I saw that the ivy had been cut down. I had lost what I intended to be my book's last photograph, or rather, it had become different.

Personal data: Born in Berlin, 1941; left in 1943, to return as a student of painting, graphic design, and photography at the Hochschule für Bildende Künste, 1960–1965.

Lived in Barcelona 1966–1973; worked as designer with Harnden & Bombelli for the pavilion "Man and His Health" for Expo '67 in Montreal, then as free-lance photographer of architecture, mainly with Ricardo Bofill.

Stayed in New York 1969–1973; worked with Herb Lubalin,

designing and building a construction barricade for Georg Jensen.

Worked as director of photography on first film, Robert Cordier's <u>Injun Fender</u>.

In Paris since 1973, shooting a television film about the "Taller Bofill," architects in Barcelona.

Will anyone believe that there are such houses? No, they will say I am misrepresenting. This time it is the truth, nothing omitted, and naturally nothing added. Where should I get it from? Everyone knows I am poor. Everyone knows it. Houses? But, to be precise, they were houses that were no longer there. Houses that had been pulled down from top to bottom. What was there was the other houses, those that had stood alongside of them, tall neighboring houses. Apparently these were in danger of falling down, since everything along-side had been taken away; for a whole scaffolding of long, tarred timbers had been rammed slantwise between the rubbish-strewn ground and the bared wall. I don't know whether I have already said that it is this wall I mean. But it was, so to speak, not the first wall of the existing houses (as one would have supposed), but the last of those that had been there. One saw its inner side. One saw at the different storeys the walls of rooms to which the paper still clung, and here and there the join of floor or ceiling. Beside these room-walls there still remained, along the whole length of the wall, a dirty-white area, and through this crept in unspeakably disgusting motions, worm-soft and as if digesting, the open, rust-spotted channel of the water-closet pipe. Grey, dusty traces of the paths the lighting-gas had taken remained at the ceiling edges, and here and there, quite unexpectedly, they bent sharp around and came running into the colored wall and into a hole that had been torn out black and ruthless. But most unforgettable of all were the walls themselves. The stubborn life of these rooms had not let itself be trampled out. It was still there; it clung to the nails that had been left, it stood on the remaining handsbreadth of flooring, it crouched under the corner joints where there was still a little bit of interior. One could see that it was in the paint, which, year by year, it had slowly altered: blue into moldy green, green into grey, and yellow into an old, stale, rotting white. But it was also in the spots that had kept fresher, behind mirrors, pictures, and wardrobes; for it had drawn and redrawn their contours, and had been with spiders and dust even in these hidden places that now lay bared. It was in every flayed strip, it was in the damp blisters at the lower edges of the wallpapers; it wavered in the torn-off shreds, and sweated out of the foul patches that had come into being long ago. And from these walls once blue and green and yellow, which were framed by the fracture-tracks of the demolished partitions, the breath of these lives stood out—the clammy, sluggish, musty breath, which no wind had yet scattered. There stood the middays and the sicknesses and the exhaled breath and the smoke of years, and the sweat that breaks out under armpits and makes clothes heavy, and the stale breath of mouths, and the fusel odor of sweltering feet. There stood the tang of urine and the burn of soot and the grey reek of potatoes, and the heavy, smooth stench of ageing grease. The sweet, lingering smell of neglected infants was there, and the fear-smell of children who go to school, and the sultriness out of the beds of nubile youths. To these was added much that had come from below, from the abyss of the street, which reeked, and more that had oozed down from above with the rain, which over cities is not clean. And much the feeble, tamed domestic winds, that always stay in the same street, had brought along; and much more was there, the source of which one did not know. I said, did I not, that all the walls had been demolished except the last—? It is of this wall I have been speaking all along.

Rainer Maria Rilke, **Notebooks of Malte Laurids Brigge**

Index of Places

Cover and title page photograph: Paris, avenue de Saint-Ouen, detail of pages 100–101

*Walls that don't exist any more, to my knowledge

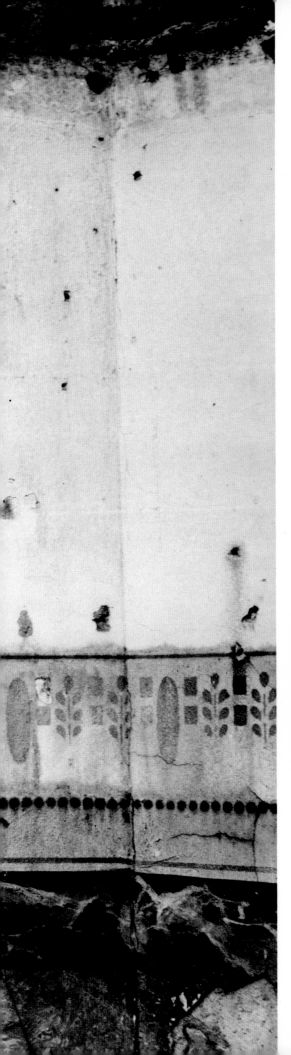

ckha

achen & Fein-Ge

von

Carl Lauterbach.

7. Motz Str. 7.

Bäckerei.

31

34

B. Palm
Milchkur-Anstalt Teleph: 141.
Pankow Schmidt-Str: 10
Kindermilch
für Anstalten u.
Haushaltungen.

CHOCOLAT SUCHARD
EN VENTE ICI
CHOCOLAT
CACAO
Suchard
97
CHOCOLAT
AU
LAIT
SUCHARD

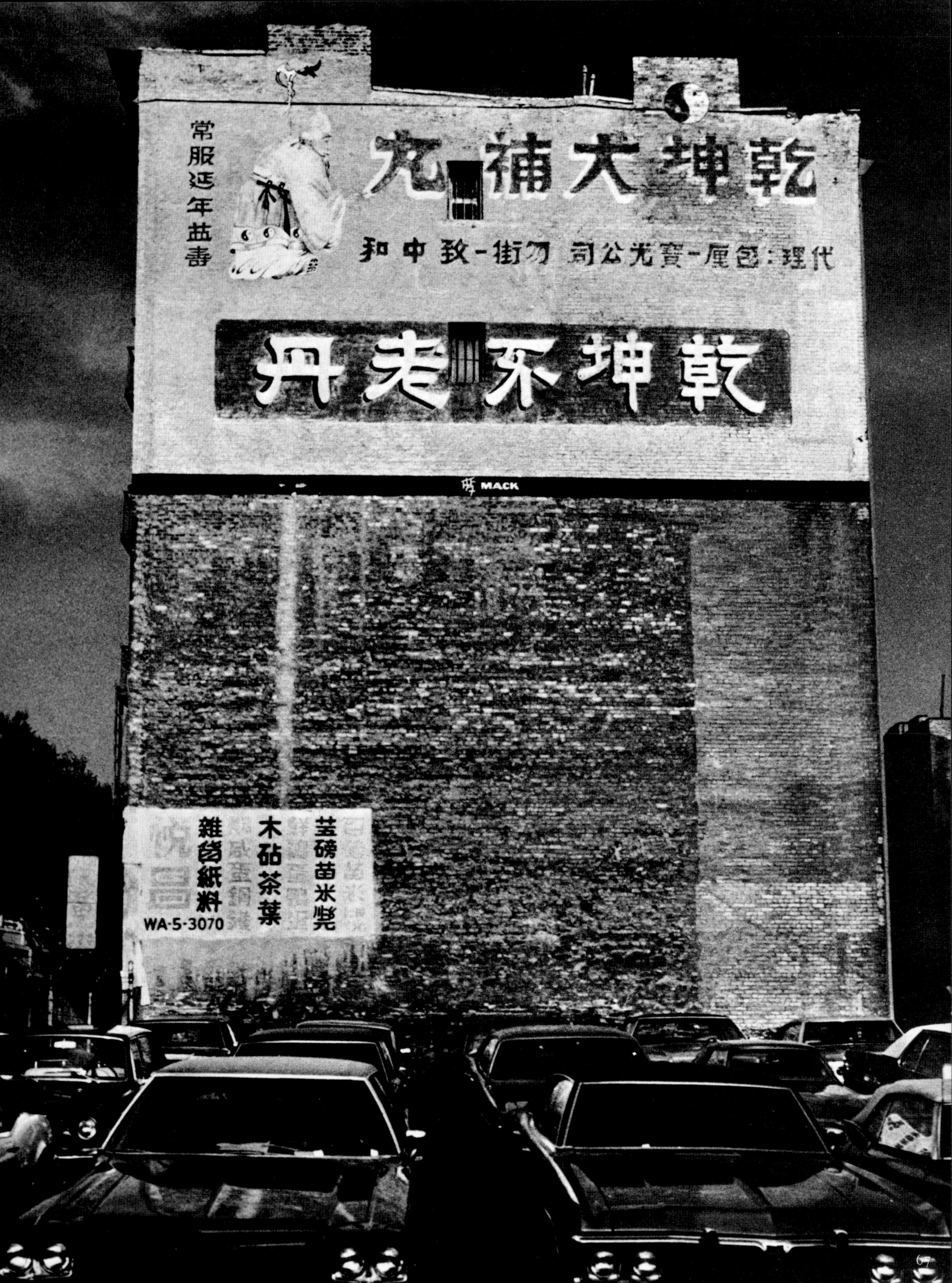
常服延年益壽
乾坤大補丸
MACK
木砧茶葉
雜貨紙料
WA-5-3070

General Outdoor

NEW & USED
MACHINE
TOOLS
GRAHAM

SEE OUR
SELECT STOCK

...Regardez
bien cette
boîte...
IMPERMEABLE
DEPOSEE
TOUTES
CHAUSSURES

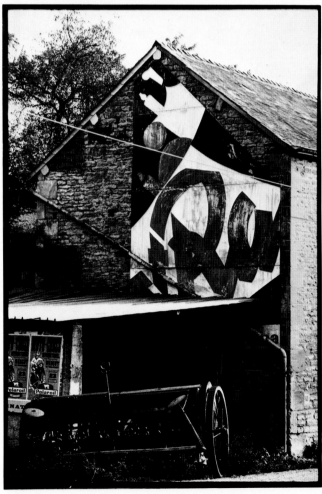

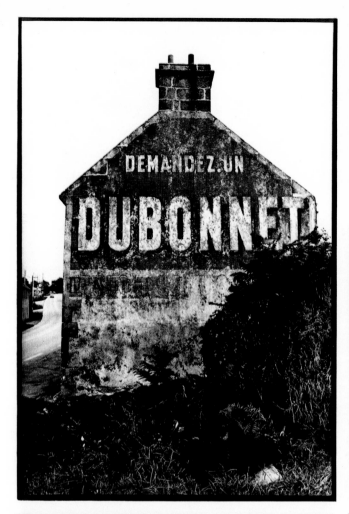

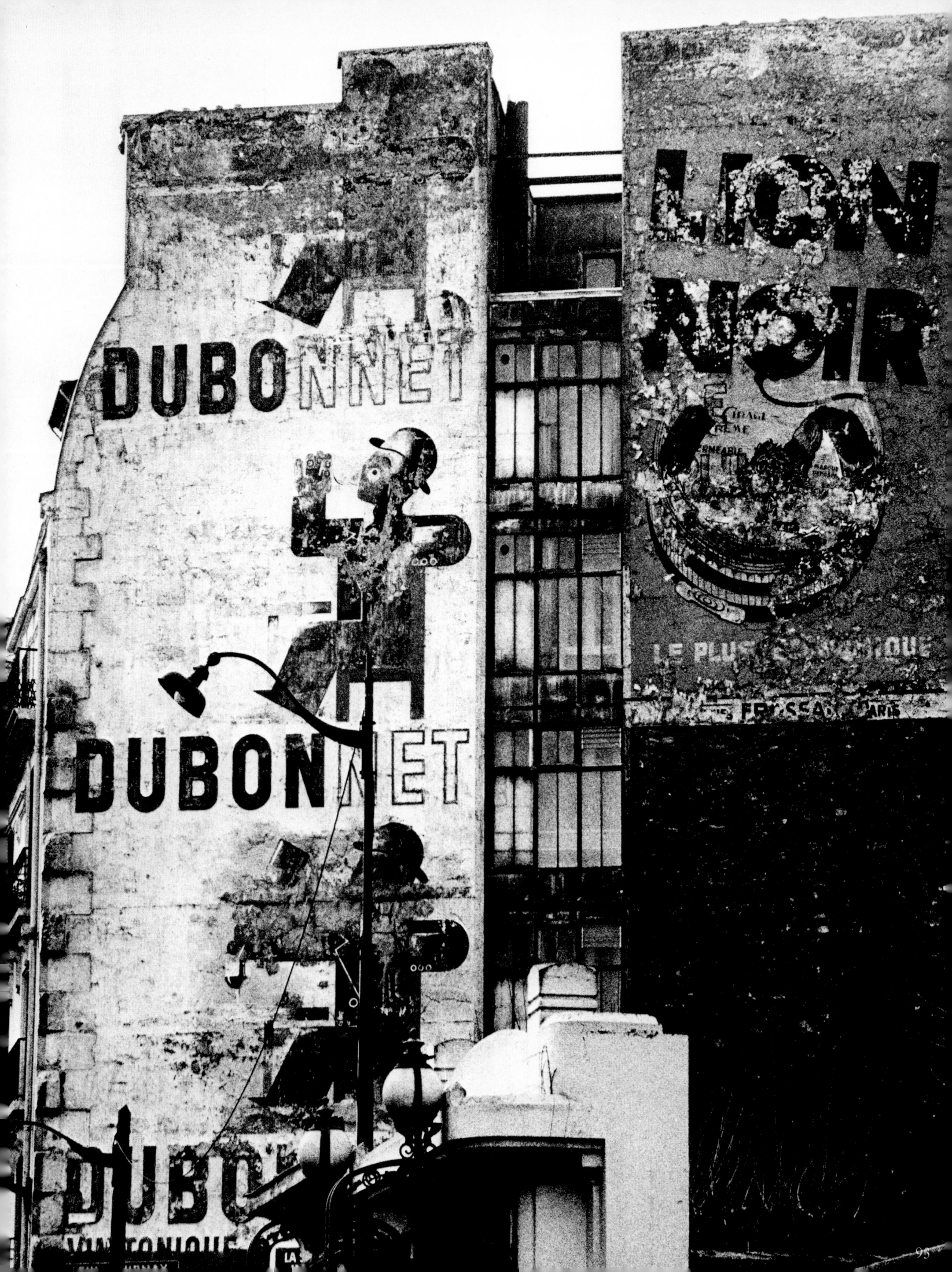
DUBONNET
DUBONNET
LION
NOIR

95

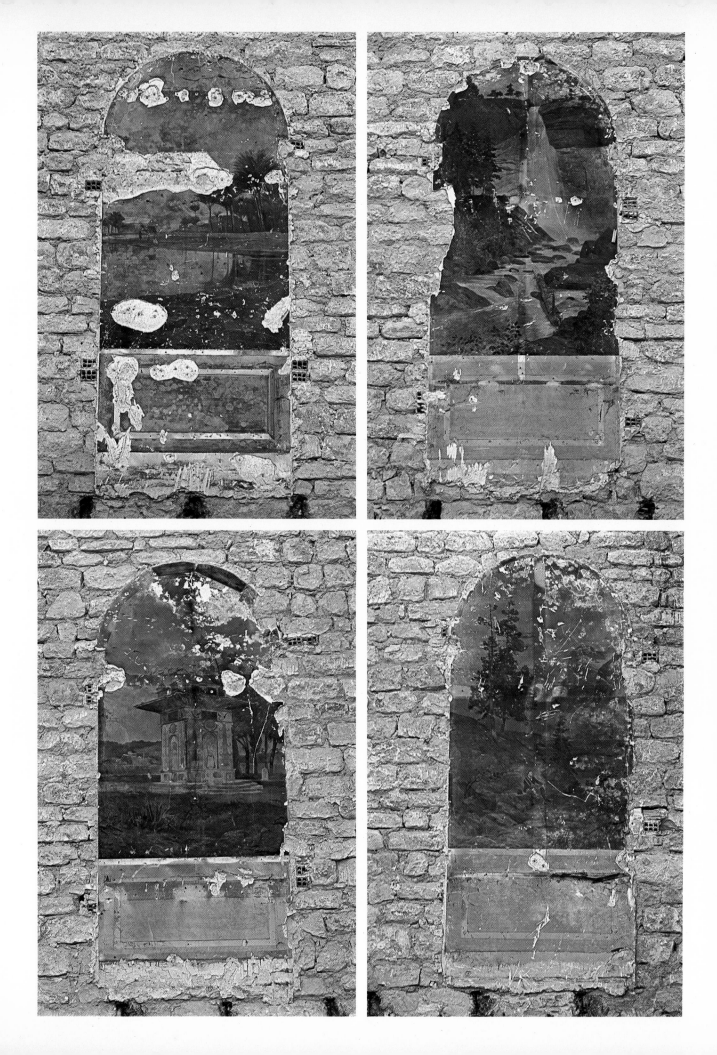

123